Workbook

EXp3 Journalism

A Handbook for Journalists

Mark Levin (Author)
Director: National Elementary Schools Press Association (NESPA)
Adviser: newspaper
Carolina Day School
Asheville, NC

Richard P. Johns (Senior Consultant)
Executive Director: Quill and Scroll Society
School of Journalism and Mass Communication
The University of Iowa
Iowa City, IA

Kaye Bird (Reviewer)
Adviser: newspaper
Indiana Junior High School
Indiana, PA

Michele Dunaway (Reviewer)
Co-chairperson: Journalism Education Association (JEA)
Middle/Junior High School Commission
Adviser: newspaper and news broadcasts
Rockwood South Middle School
Fenton, MO

Pat S. Graff (Reviewer)
Liaison: Journalism Education Association (JEA)/ National Council of Teachers of English (NCTE)
Adviser: newspaper, radio/TV news broadcasts, and literary magazine
La Cueva High School
Albuquerque, NM

Brian Martinez (Reviewer)
Adviser: newspaper and yearbook
McCullough Junior High School
The Woodlands, TX

Mark Sherwood (Reviewer)
Adviser: yearbook
Milwe Middle School
Longwood, FL

Workbook

Journalism

A Handbook for Journalists

National Textbook Company
a division of NTC/Contemporary Publishing Group
Lincolnwood, Illinois USA

Interior and cover design: Grenier Design Associates

Interior and cover illustrations: Scott Matthews

ISBN 0-8442-2246-1

Published by National Textbook Company,
a division of NTC/Contemporary Publishing Group, Inc.
4255 West Touhy Avenue
Lincolnwood (Chicago), Illinois 60712-1975 U.S.A.

Manufactured in the United States of America.

4 5 6 7 8 9 10 047 11 10 09 08 07

Contents

Chapter 4

Types of Journalistic Writing

Chapter 5

Copyediting and Proofreading

Chapter 6

Design and Production

Chapter 7

Photojournalism

Chapter 8

Business and Advertising

Chapter 9

Ethics and Responsibilities

Chapter 10

Beyond the School Newspaper

Name: ______________________ Date: ____________

1.1 Newspaper Staff Duties

Review the duties involved in each newspaper staff position. Then complete the exercises that follow on page 3.

Editor-in-Chief

- assumes responsibility for the newspaper, its staff, and its content
- represents the newspaper to the community and to the adviser
- serves as a link between the adviser and the staff
- performs duties of other staff members, as needed, to ensure the best possible publication
- oversees each issue of the newspaper
- calls meetings of the editorial board and acts as its chairperson
- works with the adviser to fill key staff positions
- makes overall decisions about the newspaper's content
- makes decisions regarding space available for each newspaper section
- takes charge of the editorial page and column writers
- works with section editors and the design editor to assign stories, photographs, and illustrations
- helps settle disputes among staff members

Section Editors

- keep well informed on topics relevant to their assigned sections
- advise and train reporters
- make story assignments
- write stories when necessary
- work with reporters to polish stories
- help proofread their sections

Copy Editors

- check all copy before it goes into the pages to make sure it's accurate and conforms to the newspaper's rules for grammar, punctuation, and word usage
- help reporters and editors improve their copy

Reporters

- find stories to cover
- keep up-to-date on what's going on in the community and in the world
- gather information through research and interviews
- write stories
- take photographs if no photographer is available

Name: ______________________________ Date: ______________

1.1 Newspaper Staff Duties (continued)

Design Editor

- plans the overall design of the newspaper
- supervises the design staff
- works with the editor-in-chief and section editors to assign photographs and illustrations
- makes assignments to artists as needed
- supervises the production of the newspaper

Design Staff

- creates visually interesting and exciting pages
- places articles, illustrations, photos, and ads according to the planned page design
- prepares final pages for printing or photocopying

Photographers

- shoot and develop photos as assigned
- get photo releases when needed *(Handbook,* p. 177)
- gather information for cutlines *(Handbook,* p. 72)
- help maintain a file of all photos and negatives taken for the publication

Business Manager

- with the adviser, manages financial accounts for the newspaper
- coordinates fundraising
- supervises advertising staff
- bills advertisers
- works with the design editor to determine the number of pages for each issue

Advertising Staff

- sells advertising space for each issue
- writes ad copy
- designs and prepares ads

Circulation Manager

- prepares newspapers for distribution
- keeps distribution files up-to-date
- bills subscribers *(Handbook,* p. 205)
- prints mailing labels
- makes assignments to staff for distribution

Name: ______________________________ Date: ____________

1.1 Newspaper Staff Duties (continued)

A. Think about the different duties of each position on the newspaper staff. Answer the following questions by telling which positions would be the best fit for each skill and/or personality trait.

1. Which positions require very detail-oriented people?

____

2. Which positions require people with strong visual and/or artistic skills?

____

3. Which positions require skill at working well with the public?

____

4. Which positions require an ability to work with numbers?

____

5. Which positions require strong problem-solving skills?

____

B. Now think about your own skills and talents. Write a paragraph about which position you feel you would be most suited to and why.

____

____

____

____

____

____

Name: ______________________________ Date: ______________

1.2 Your Newspaper Team

In the space below, draw a diagram of your school newspaper's organization. Show the chain of command, from the publisher (adviser) downward. You can use the diagram on page 7 of the *Handbook* as a guide, or you can make up your own graphic. Under the name of each position in your diagram, write some of the specific duties required by staff on your newspaper team. You may need to check with individual members of your newspaper team to see how their duties vary from those mentioned in the *Handbook*.

Name: ______________________________ Date: ______________

1.3 Evaluating Readership

A. Look at the lists of stories below taken from three newspapers. Based on the topics of the stories, write at least two things you can assume about each newspaper's readership.

1. *The Bedford Sentinel*
   Mayor heads up anti-litter campaign
   Community activist to speak at rally
   Vandalism rates rise in Brentley Park area
   Pollution: a growing local problem
   Governor demands stricter car-seat laws

   ____

   ____

2. *The Sun Haven Times*
   Lower auto insurance rates please older drivers
   Local charity group seeks volunteers
   Flu shots a must, says local doctor
   Mall walking linked to better health
   St. Matthew's cancels Sunday pancake breakfasts

   ____

   ____

3. *The Glass Lake Mirror*
   Class play breaks attendance records
   Former Glass Lake debater wins senate race
   Intramural volleyball tournament planned
   Artists chosen for cafeteria mural
   Driver's ed courses expanded to include boat driving

   ____

   ____

Name: ______________________________ Date: ____________

1.3 Evaluating Readership (continued)

B. Review a recent issue of your school paper and another local paper. Take notes on what these publications tell you about their readers. Document the information that leads to your inferences.

Your school newspaper: ____________________ Publication date: __________

Story title: ____________________ Page number: __________

The readers of this newspaper ______________________________

Story title: ____________________ Page number: __________

The readers of this newspaper ______________________________

Story title: ____________________ Page number: __________

The readers of this newspaper ______________________________

Your local newspaper: ____________________ Publication date: __________

Story title: ____________________ Page number: __________

The readers of this newspaper ______________________________

Story title: ____________________ Page number: __________

The readers of this newspaper ______________________________

Story title: ____________________ Page number: __________

The readers of this newspaper ______________________________

Name: ______________________ Date: ____________

1.4 Charting the Process

A. Draw a flowchart of your newspaper's process, from the first staff meeting through distribution of the finished paper. Make sure it's clear what is happening at each stage. Take special care to show which actions happen at the same time and which happen in a particular sequence.

Name: ______________________________ Date: ____________

1.4 Charting the Process (continued)

B. In a small group, discuss any possible weak links within your paper's production process. How might these areas be strengthened to better serve the paper as a whole? Write your ideas below.

Name: ______________________________ Date: ______________

2.1 Determining Newsworthiness

A. Look at the list of topics below. On the line following each topic, write each element of news (timeliness, human interest, proximity, prominence, consequence, and conflict) that makes the topic newsworthy to readers of your *school* newspaper. If it contains none, write "Not newsworthy." Explain your answers as necessary.

1. A nuclear power plant four miles from your area that has just been cited for code violations

   ____

2. A student at your school who has returned to school after overcoming cancer

   ____

3. A storm six weeks ago that knocked out electricity in town for a day

   ____

4. An upcoming visit to an area college by the President of the United States

   ____

B. Now write a story topic for readers of your *local* newspaper that illustrates each of the following elements of news:

5. Timeliness: ______________________________

6. Human interest: ______________________________

7. Proximity: ______________________________

8. Prominence: ______________________________

9. Consequence: ______________________________

10. Conflict: ______________________________

Name: ______________________________ Date: ______________

2.2 Hard News or Soft News?

A. Read the story topics below. Decide whether each topic is most likely hard news or soft news. Circle your choice.

1.	The wide variety of area jobs for students	Hard	Soft
2.	A 32-cent increase in the minimum wage	Hard	Soft
3.	Results of a survey on motorcycle safety and helmet laws	Hard	Soft
4.	A popular teacher's recent death in a motorcycle accident	Hard	Soft
5.	Plans for a new mall to go up three blocks from the school	Hard	Soft
6.	Shopping malls: their long and interesting history	Hard	Soft

B. Clip two examples of soft news and two examples of hard news from your school or local paper. On the lines below, explain your reasons for classifying each story as you did. Label and staple the clippings to this worksheet.

Hard-news story #1: ______________________________

____

Hard-news story #2: ______________________________

____

Soft-news story #1: ______________________________

____

Soft-news story #2: ______________________________

____

Name: ______________________ Date: ____________

2.3 Primary Sources and Secondary Sources

A. Look at the story excerpts below. Decide whether the information in each excerpt most likely came from a primary or a secondary source. Explain your answer.

> Parental advisory laws have been in effect since 1990, and the punishment for not enforcing those laws is strict. For example, in 1991 a store clerk in Florida was arrested for selling a stickered album to a minor.
>
> (From the *Rockwood South Rampage,* November 30, 1998, Rockwood South Middle School, Fenton, MO)

1. ______________________

____

> Trivia players, newscasters for CNN, investigative reporters, and buyers of souvenirs. The English Festival Team was this and much more during their visit to the Newseum, an interactive museum in Washington, D.C.
>
> (From the *Crimson Arrow,* May 8, 1998, Indiana Junior High, Indiana, PA)

2. ______________________

____

> Overall, the players were satisfied with the win, although some players believe there is still room for improvement. "We didn't do as well as planned, but it was a big improvement because it was our first win of the season," said Do Kim, junior.
>
> (From *The Epitaph,* December 18, 1998, Homestead High School, Cupertino, CA)

3. ______________________

____

Name: ______________________________ Date: ______________

2.3 Primary Sources and Secondary Sources (continued)

B. Imagine that you have been assigned to write a feature article on students who are involved in an area Civil War reenactment. You intend to provide background information on teenagers who fought in the Civil War. On the lines below list three specific primary sources and three specific secondary sources you might use to find the information you need. Evaluate your sources, especially those you find on the Internet, to ensure they are reliable and current.

Primary Sources:

____

____

____

Secondary Sources:

____

____

____

Name: ____________________ Date: __________

2.4 Stories and Sources Scavenger Hunt

Over the next 24 hours, find as many newsworthy stories for your school newspaper in each of the general categories listed on this page and the next page. Look for stories in your school, local community, and global community that your readers may want or need to know. List potential sources for each story idea you provide. If you get a tip for a story, name the source of the tip.

Art:

____

____

____

Environment:

____

____

____

Fashion:

____

____

____

Food:

____

____

____

Name: ______________________________ Date: ______________

2.4 Stories and Sources Scavenger Hunt (continued)

Health:

____

____

____

History:

____

____

____

Music:

____

____

____

Recreation:

____

____

____

Technology:

____

____

____

Name: ______________________________ Date: ______________

2.5 Angles

Working in pairs or small groups, brainstorm angles your newspaper might take on each of the topics listed below and on the following page. Include ideas for localizing each angle.

Pets:

____

____

____

Astrology:

____

____

____

Vegetarianism:

____

____

____

Presidential Elections:

____

____

____

Name: ______________________________ Date: ______________

2.5 Angles (continued)

Computer Animation:

____

____

____

Racism:

____

____

____

Self-defense:

____

____

____

World Hunger:

____

____

____

Name: ______________________________ Date: ______________

2.6 Interview Questions

Read the story below. Imagine you wrote the story. On the next page, write a list of 10 questions you asked during your interviews to get the information in the story. Identify to whom you asked each question—students, teachers, or students and teachers.

Eighth-grade students fight taxation in American History

by Danielle Zanella, Staff Reporter

Enraged protestors boomed into Room 27 on a day in October shouting out phrases written on the signs they waved about. "No taxation without representation!" "Burn the bungalow!" "Davis's candy stash deserves a tax!" What exactly was this all about?

Mr. Lenard Davis, eighth-grade history teacher, had been charging students a penny for homework assignments, and stamping them, similar to the stamp tax of 1764.

Davis, along with another eighth-grade history teacher, Mr. David Chee, demanded a Quartering Act whereby the colonists had to house British soldiers: Students with pictures of soldiers taped to their desks had to pay one penny each day the soldiers "lived" with them.

In another occurrence, some students purchased tea bags for a penny. Then the students threw the tea on the floor reenacting the events of the Boston Tea Party.

When students in Davis's fourth period history class became angered over this and protested, the taxes were stopped and afterwards students received a "prison sentence," all in fun, of course.

Roxanne Niksch, who took part organizing this raid, said the taxes were not right, even if it was only a penny.

The teachers' responses? Davis said it helps the students to understand history. Chee said, "I think the students feel the inconvenience that the colonists felt having British soldiers stay in their homes."

As for the pennies, students will soon become "members of the Senate" and determine how to spend the money and then pass a bill in Congress to do so.

(From the *Tiger's Tale,* November 13, 1997, MacArthur Intermediate School, Santa Ana, CA)

Name: ______________________________ Date: ______________

2.6 Interview Questions (continued)

Interview Questions:

1. ______________________________
2. ______________________________
3. ______________________________
4. ______________________________
5. ______________________________
6. ______________________________
7. ______________________________
8. ______________________________
9. ______________________________
10. ______________________________

Name: ______________________________ Date: ______________

2.7 The Interview Process

A. Imagine you have been granted an interview with a celebrity. Research this person and then write a list of at least 10 questions you will ask, in the order in which you would ask them. Document your research.

Celebrity:

____

Interview Questions:

____

____

____

____

____

____

____

____

____

____

Research Resources:

____

____

____

____

Name: ____ Date: ________________

2.7 The Interview Process (continued)

B. Work with another student to role-play the interview process, including scheduling the interview. Interview your partner, who will portray the celebrity you chose in Part A of this worksheet. Use your prepared interview questions. Then switch places and have your partner interview you as you portray his or her celebrity. Make sure you research your partner's celebrity to be prepared to play that role. But don't rehearse the role-plays.

Ask your partner and your classmates to evaluate you on your interviewing skills. Use the space below to assess yourself, incorporating helpful suggestions from your classmates.

Name: ______________________ Date: ____________

3.1 Accuracy and Objectivity

A. Read the sentences below. In each sentence, underline which information you would double-check for accuracy. On the line following each sentence, write what sources you could use to check the information.

1. Lily Morales, 9th grade, was born blind.

   ____

2. She has written a play, *"A Través de Mis Ojos"* (Spanish for "Through my Eyes") about what it's like to be a blind Hispanic teenager.

   ____

3. She will perform a scene from her play for the Talent Show on May 18.

   ____

4. Morales attended the Carroll School for the Blind in Portland, Oregon, for 12 years before coming to Drummond Junior High.

   ____

5. Morales has an Alaskan Malamute guide dog named after the Roman god of light, Jupiter.

   ____

B. Underline any editorializing in the following sentences:

1. Justin Sveboda, 8th grade, is the only contestant in the county to qualify for the regional skateboarding competition.
2. Because everyone likes ice cream—especially when it's hot, the pom squad will sell sundaes at their noon bake sales during the month of May.
3. The national parks of America are national treasures.
4. Book clubs are suddenly springing up all over in response to Oprah Winfrey's entertaining book chats on her TV talk show.
5. Reid Yang's talented TV production students produced a telethon last weekend.

Name: ______________________________ Date: ______________

3.2 Clear, Concise, and Colorful Writing

A. Rewrite each of the sentences below to make them clear, concise, and colorful. You may choose to divide an example into more than one sentence.

1. There are three new faces in the faculty lounge this year.

____

2. Last year students included gang-related signs in their murals, which is against school policy, so this year Liana Koa, social studies teacher, told students involved in the mural project that it was absolutely necessary to get final approval from her for all designs before commencing with their murals.

____

____

3. Faulty wiring in a pottery kiln was blamed by firefighters for the art room fire that destroyed everything.

____

4. It was agreed by all student council members to cease putting up decorations related to religious holiday celebrations in order to avoid offending students whose religious holidays might not be represented.

____

____

5. After a slow start in the junior rowing regatta, Sherri Laredo, 6th grade, sailed ahead of everyone to steal the show with a first-place finish.

____

B. Read a newspaper story of at least five paragraphs. Underline the transitions in the story. Then cut the story apart into paragraphs. Number the paragraphs in order on the back of each. Using the logical flow of the story, see if you can put the story back together (without looking at the numbers). Tape the story back together and attach it to this worksheet.

Name: ______________________________ Date: ______________

3.3 Analyzing Leads

A. Read each of the leads below. On the lines following each example, write which type of lead it is—a summary lead, scenic lead, storytelling lead, punch lead, opposite lead, or blind lead. Some may be a combination of types.

> A West Franklin graduate celebrated his twenty-first birthday on May 2 with friends. The next day his parents identified him at the county morgue.
>
> Jeremy Albright had always been a careful driver. But shortly after 1 a.m. on May 3, after hours of excessive drinking, he lost control of his car and slammed into a tree. He died at Lourdes Memorial Hospital two hours later.

1. ____

> The object of any competition is to win, says computer gamer Josh Bartlett, 6th grade. Collin Hoyt, 7th grade, says he plays computer games "to test my own skills and have fun with my buddies."

2. ____

> The school needs a new gymnasium by the year 2003, Delton school board superintendent Quinn Majors told parents and teachers at the May 25 town meeting.

3. ____

Name: ______________________________ Date: ______________

3.3 Analyzing Leads (continued)

> Like a thundering herd of buffalo, their breath clouding in the night air and their cleats clattering on the pavement, the varsity football team burst out of the locker room.
>
> At halftime, with the scoreboard spelling defeat, the team staggered back into the locker room. Even the Homecoming crowd's cheers of encouragement couldn't raise their spirits.

4. ______________________________

B. Read the question and quote leads below. If they satisfy the requirements for these types of leads as described on page 47 of the *Handbook,* explain why. If they don't, rewrite them as another type of lead.

> Is cheating a problem at Clayton Middle School? In a recent student survey, 80 percent of students said they have cheated at least once on school work. Another 17 percent said they cheat regularly. Only 3 percent said they have never cheated.

5. ______________________________

____

> "Danger walks our streets," announced self-proclaimed "crime buster" Todd Levertow at a rally on June 8 in the school gym.
>
> Parents, students, and other members of the community packed the gym, which was decorated with FBI-type "Wanted" posters and large signs stating crime figures.

6. ______________________________

____

Name: ____________________ Date: __________

3.4 Writing and Rewriting Leads

A. Using the following facts, write one summary lead and one creative lead on the lines below:

- Absences increased 10 percent above normal in the past month.
- The increase is due to flu.
- More than 150 students have missed school due to illness from the flu.
- This strain of flu lasts three or four days.
- Symptoms include sore throat, coughing, runny nose, nausea, headache, and sometimes a fever.
- To prevent catching the flu, school nurse Belinda Henning advises students to eat a well-balanced diet, drink plenty of water and juice, get a good night's sleep, wash hands frequently, and avoid sharing beverages.
- Sick students have been lining up at the school nurse's office.
- Because of the flu, Henning spends half of her day calling parents to pick up sick students and the other half handing out aspirin.

Summary Lead:

____

____

____

Creative Lead:

____

____

____

Name: ______________________________________ Date: ________________

3.4 Writing and Rewriting Leads (continued)

B. Read the lead below and the facts on which it was based. Rewrite the lead to make it better. Try several versions. Attach all of your versions to this worksheet, marking the one you like best.

> Imagine traveling to China to meet your relatives for the first time. That's what Melinda Lee, 9th grade, did last month.
>
> She and her family flew into Hong Kong and then took another plane and three buses to the mountain village of their relatives. Everyone hugged and cried. Lee's parents hadn't seen their families in 17 years.

- Melinda Lee, 9th grade, met her grandparents, aunts and uncles, and cousins for the first time last month.
- All her relatives live in mountain villages near Chungking in the Szechwan province of China, which is in the central part of the nation.
- Lee went with her parents and two little brothers to visit them for two weeks.
- Lee's parents left China for the United States after their marriage 17 years ago and had not been back since.
- Lee's relatives in China are farmers and miners.
- Lee's family had been saving for several years to go to China.
- Lee's family took a plane to Hong Kong, another plane to Chunking, and then took three buses to reach the area where her relatives live.
- Everyone hugged and cried when they saw each other.
- One of Lee's grandmothers made her a traditional Chinese quilted jacket.
- The climate in the mountains is much colder than in Southern California, where Lee and her family live.
- During her visit, Lee went to a traditional open-air market, explored several caves with her cousins, and ate some very spicy Szechwan meals.

Name: ______________________________ Date: ______________

3.5 Direct Quotes to Indirect Quotes

On the lines below, paraphrase each of the following direct quotes, creating an indirect quote or a partial quote. Include attribution as necessary. (Be careful not to misquote.)

1. "I'd like to stress that snakes are not evil creatures," the zoologist said. "They contribute to the environment and have a purpose in it, just as you do. In fact, they probably do more good for the environment than humans do."

   ____

   ____

2. Principal Miguel Herrerra said, "Students are either proud of their school or they aren't. It's important to show pride in yourself and your school. You show pride through your behavior—your respect for others and your respect for yourself."

   ____

   ____

3. "All right," said one of the actors in the touring play, "we want a few volunteers to take the stage and show us what the students of Mullavey Middle School are really made of!"

   ____

   ____

4. Police officer Joe Chin said, "Accidents like this happen all the time. The driver is traveling at too high a rate of speed, the condition of the road is icy, and the car spins out of control. People have got to slow down on these roads in winter."

   ____

   ____

5. "Why, there's no stronger team in this conference," said Coach Dana Little. "Our record speaks for itself. I think we have an excellent shot at the division title this year."

   ____

   ____

Name: ______________________________ Date: ______________

3.6 Checking Attribution

Read the story below. Then do the following:

- Underline the attributions for the direct quotes.
- Draw two lines under the attributions for indirect quotes, including partial quotes.
- Place a checkmark at the beginning of sentences that are indirect quotes that don't require attribution; that is, they are statements based on facts the reporter got from a source.
- If you think any statement needs an attribution but doesn't have one, place a question mark next to it.

Trouble's Brewing on Bus #51

by Kassy Korobkova

Every day crowds of students wait at the bus stop on Helena Avenue for Bus #51.

According to Vice Principal Liz Adams, yelling and the fighting happen because of the crowding.

Fights are not the only problem on #51's route. Once a seventh-grader, not wanting to wait for other students to get off the bus, jumped out the window. "That's not fun, that's dangerous," commented eighth-grader Andrea Puljiz.

Lack of space is also an issue. On Sept. 30, about twelve people didn't fit in the bus and were left at the bus stop on Helena Avenue.

On Friday, Oct. 9 and Monday, Oct. 16, the bus simply didn't come. The calls of many angry parents, and the school staff, prompted the Valley Transportation Authority to respond. Too many drivers hadn't shown up to work.

Fights happen on the bus almost daily. Adams said that if the fights get worse, the bus stop will be moved from Helena back to Homestead and students will have to walk way over there.

Eighth-grader Ajene White said, "There are way too many people on the bus! We seriously need another one!"

Adams agreed. "We've talked with the Valley Transportation Authority, and hopefully, we'll resolve the problem," she said.

While the staff is trying to "resolve the problem," the line to the bus continues to grow.

(From *The Cupertino Chronicle,* November 23, 1998, Cupertino Junior High School, Sunnyvale, CA)

Name: ______________________________ Date: ______________

3.7 Story Formats

Imagine the facts below are summarized from your interview and research notes for a story. On the next page, write a story based on these facts. You may use the inverted-pyramid format with a summary lead or the storytelling format with a creative lead.

- Fiona Malloy and Royce Franklin, both 7th graders, participate in Tae Kwon Do.
- This summer Malloy and Franklin will compete at the Junior Olympics in Sacramento, CA.
- To go to the Junior Olympics, they had to place at least eighth in a state qualifications tournament, held in Minneapolis last month.
- Malloy and Franklin are students at the Martial Arts Center, 334 Loon Lake Rd.
- Their instructor is Larry Chang.
- "It's not about beating up people," said Chang. "It's about self-discipline, self-defense, and self-respect.
- "The three hours a day that I practice might seem like a lot, but I'm healthy and I feel great," said Franklin.
- "I love to compete," said Malloy. "I've made lots of friends at the competitions and we keep in touch with e-mail."
- Tae Kwon Do is a martial art that is widely practiced as a sport.
- Martial arts are used for combat and self-defense.
- Tae Kwon Do consists of form, which is a set of moves put together, and sparring, which is fighting with control and gear.
- Tae Kwon Do uses powerful kicking techniques.
- "The first time I executed a kick I thought I would rip my pants! It's amazing how quickly I got better," said Malloy.
- Tae Kwon Do students earn belts of different colors to indicate their skill level. Black is the highest of nine belts.
- After belts, students earn "dans." Like belts, there are nine dans.
- Malloy has been doing Tae Kwon Do for five years. She has a red belt. Her next belt is black.
- Franklin has been doing Tae Kwon Do for three years. He has a purple belt, which is three belts from a black belt.

Name: ______________________________ Date: ______________

3.7 Story Formats (continued)

Name: ______________________________ Date: ______________

3.8 Writing and Rewriting Headlines

A. Read the story below. On the next page write three possible headlines for the story. You can use upstyle or downstyle, but whichever style you choose, use it in every example. Make at least one of your headlines a kicker, hammerhead, or tripod.

For top student musicians, it's a dream gig

by Phat X. Chiem, Tribune Staff Writer

Ever since Paula Wills began learning to play the alto saxophone seven years ago, she has dreamed about performing in that elegant auditorium known as Orchestra Hall, home to the Chicago Symphony Orchestra (CSO).

On Saturday afternoon, Wills got her big chance. The recent Mother McCauley High School graduate played with the All-City High School Jazz Band, one of six performing groups that participated in the Chicago Public Schools' 36th annual All-City Festival Concert at Orchestra Hall.

The festival brought together 462 of the best musicians and choir singers from elementary and high schools throughout Chicago. Playing to a packed house, the young talents showcased a variety of musical styles, from jazz to classical, pop and gospel. For Wills, who aspires to be a professional jazz performer, the event was an unbelievable realization of a year-long ambition.

"On my list of things to do before I die was to play in Orchestra Hall," said Wills, 18, while practicing backstage a few hours before show time. "I've seen Wynton Marsalis and Keith Jarrett play here, and it's amazing to be sitting on the same stage."

Beginning in October and ending in June, the All-City groups rehearse for about two hours every Saturday. The students, who must audition to play in the festival, pay no fees and receive no extra credit. The conductors are Chicago public school teachers who are paid a nominal stipend for rehearsal and concert time.

The groups are a high school jazz band, marching band and chorus, along with an elementary school band and chorus, and a youth orchestra. On Saturday, the students also performed with a dance troupe from the Beasley Academic Center and Larry Combs, the CSO's principal clarinetist.

All the performers came together for the exuberant finale: John Williams' "Dry Your Tears, Afrika" from the movie "Amistad."

"We're going beyond just the music with this festival," conductor William A. Johnson, an instrumental music specialist for the school system, said during a brief break. "We're exposing them to an experience that will last them into their lives."

(From the *Chicago Tribune,* May 16, 1999, Chicago, IL)

Name: ______________________________ Date: ______________

3.8 Writing and Rewriting Headlines (continued)

Headline #1:

Headline #2:

Headline #3:

B. Read the following headlines, which are unintentionally funny. Rewrite each so they make sense. In some cases, you may only need to change a word or two. Try to keep them about the same length.

1. **Safety experts say school bus passengers should be belted**

   ____

2. **Stolen painting found by tree**

   ____

3. **Red tape holds up new bridge**

   ____

4. **Kids make nutritious snacks**

   ____

5. **Local high school dropouts cut in half**

   ____

Name: ______________________ Date: ____________

3.9 Writing Cutlines

A. Look at the photo below and the relevant facts that were gathered about the photo. Then write a cutline for it. Your cutline should be no more than 40 words long.

PHOTO BY BRIAN LOGSDON

- who: Rachel Thompson, 11th grade
- what: building a popsicle-stick bridge, which students will test for strength by piling on weights
- why: to earn extra credit for James Jorsch's physics class

____

____

____

____

____

Name: ______________________________ Date: ______________

3.9 Writing Cutlines (continued)

B. Find an active, quality photo of your family or friends. Tape a photocopy of the photo here. Write a cutline for the photo below it. Before writing your cutline, analyze the photo, as described on page 72 of the *Handbook*. As an extra challenge, you may choose to write a story cutline (if the photo can stand as a story in itself) or create a photo essay. If you decide to do a photo essay, use a larger sheet of paper.

Name: ______________________________ Date: ______________

4.1 News Coverage

Read the news briefs on the next two pages. Imagine that you have to condense them to make room for other news. Below each news brief, rewrite it as either a shorter news brief of only a few sentences, or as a one- or two-sentence item in a roving reporter.

News Brief #1

Model UN

by Brittany Ellenburg

Model United Nations (UN) team members study a country of their choice all year to prepare for competition on Feb. 18–19 at Georgia Southern University.

During the competition students will act as representatives from their country and discuss world issues with other students who are representing other countries. Awards will be given for how well they represent their country. Middle schoolers will be competing against high schoolers.

Model UN director Nancy Donny believes the team is well prepared.

"I think that wc havc a good chancc against thc high schoolers," Donny said.

Five awards will be given. In the past, Donny's teams have always received at least one award.

(From *The Silver and Green Gazette,* February 12, 1999, Dutch Fork Middle School, Irmo, SC)

____

____

____

____

____

Name: ______________________________ Date: ______________

4.1 News Coverage (continued)

News Brief #2

Scholastic Art Award

by Pearl Hwang

Competing with more than 3,000 art entries across the state, three CEHS students were presented with scholastic Gold and Silver Key awards.

Juniors Monique Pritz and Gina Niespodziani were each awarded Silver Key awards, and sophomore Ryogu Takeuchi was nominated as a Gold Key finalist.

"I was very surprised when I found out that I won because last year I didn't win, and I was competing against so many people," Pritz said.

The Silver Key award is a state accolade. The winner of the award receives a small silver medallion. Those who win Gold Key awards will be entered in a nationwide competition in New York City.

The artwork of those who won Silver Key awards was displayed at the University of Indianapolis last week.

(From *The Oracle,* February 19, 1999, Columbus East High School, Columbus, IN)

____

____

____

____

____

____

Name: ______________________________________ Date: ______________

4.2 Student Achievement Story

Read the facts listed below. Then do some research on the play named: its theme, author, background, and so on. On the next page, write a student achievement story based on the facts and on your research. Include a quick-read menu that lists the cast members. Make sure you follow the guidelines on page 80 of the *Handbook* for listing student names. Give your story a headline.

- The cast for the fall play, *R.U.R.* by Karel Capek, has been chosen.
- *R.U.R.* will be performed Nov. 18–21 in Lillian James Auditorium.
- The production team, formed in early September, is as follows: Charlotte Krause, language arts teacher, is the director. Bill Beck, theatre arts teacher, is the technical director. Abby Cahill, 12th grade, is the set designer. Gail Zimmer, 10th grade, is the makeup and costume designer. Seth Burns, 11th grade, is the lighting and sound designer.
- Krause said, "We have an experienced and talented cast who are eager to begin work on this amazing play, which has a very relevant theme for our age of machines and inventions."
- Cahill said, "The production team has been busy designing the show for several weeks. It's going to look superfuturistic."
- Burns said, "We're going to use lots of multimedia—computers, TVs, projections."
- The cast of characters is as follows: Greg Lewellyn, 12th grade, is Harry Domain, General Manager for R.U.R. Toni Workman, 10th grade, is Fabry, Chief Engineer for R.U.R. Jeff Tigh, 12th grade, is Dr. Gall, Head of the Physiological Dept. of R.U.R. Reed Petrowski, 11th grade, is Dr. Hellman, Psychologist-in-Chief. Karl Sweet, 9th grade, is Jacob Berman, Managing Director of R.U.R. Dirk Schneider, 10th grade, is Alquist, Clerk of the Works of R.U.R. Natasha Kohl, 11th grade, is Helena Glory. Lucy Forge, 9th grade, is Nana, her maid. Pat Wolfe, 11th grade, is Marius, a robot. Erin Jensen, 10th grade, is Sula, a robot. Adam Dallas, 9th grade, is Radius, a robot. Wade Perth, 11th grade, is Primus, a robot. Ginger Palucci, 12th grade, is Helena, a robotess. Sara Brentano, 9th grade, is a robot servant.

Name: ______________________________ Date: ______________

4.2 Student Achievement Story (continued)

Name: ______________________________ Date: ______________

4.3 Analysis: In-depth Reporting

Read an in-depth story in your local newspaper. Then answer the questions below. Attach the story to this worksheet.

1. What is the main topic of this story?

   ____

2. Why do you think this topic was covered as an in-depth story?

   ____

3. Is the topic related to a recent news item? If so, what is the news item?

   ____

4. Is the topic "hot" (of current high interest) with readers of the newspaper?

   ____

5. Is the topic focused? Explain.

   ____

6. Does the story have a unique, localized angle? If so, what is it?

   ____

7. Does the story seem to be thoroughly researched? Name as many sources as you can find. Cite the particular paragraph(s) in which each is first identified. Classify each as primary or secondary sources.

   ____

   ____

   ____

   ____

Name: ______________________ Date: ____________

4.3 Analysis: In-depth Reporting (continued)

8. Are there at least two primary sources for each main point? If so, summarize two of the main points and list the primary sources for each. Cite the particular paragraph(s) in which each primary source is identified.

9. Does the story offer a wide range of stimulating facts and opinions? If so, name three of the most interesting. Cite the particular paragraph(s) in which each appears.

10. Does the story have a sidebar? If so, explain how the sidebar relates to or adds to the main story (or mainbar). Attach the sidebar to this worksheet.

Name: ______________________ Date: __________

4.4 Conducting a Survey

Working with three or four other students, conduct a survey on one of the following topics (or on a topic approved by your adviser):

- computers
- animal rights
- violence in the media
- extraterrestial life
- dress codes
- teen hangouts

To get a random sample, survey 10 percent of your group or 50 people, whichever is more. Try to make your random sample representative of the different ages, sexes, ethnicities, and races in your group.

For this exercise, use closed questions, since they are easier to count and organize into results. You may need to include filter questions to get relevant responses.

You may conduct your survey in person or in writing. Compute and report the results in the form of a short story or a graph or chart and attach it to this worksheet.

Group Surveyed:

____

Questions:

____

____

____

____

____

____

____

____

____

Name: ______________________________ Date: ______________

4.5 Analysis: Consumer Reporting

Read a story that serves as an example of one of the three approaches to consumer reporting: compare and contrast, bargain hunt, and consumer advocate. Then answer the questions below. Attach the story you read to this worksheet.

1. What type of consumer story did you read?

   ____

2. What product or service does the story cover?

   ____

3. Summarize the story's factual conclusions about the product or service in terms of concerns such as cost, safety, service, performance, and quality.

   ____

   ____

   ____

   ____

4. What does the writer recommend that consumers do, if anything?

   ____

   ____

5. Is the story well researched? Explain, naming sources cited in the story.

   ____

   ____

6. Is the story objective? Explain.

   ____

   ____

Name: ______________________________ Date: ______________

4.6 Analysis: Features

Read a newspaper feature story. Then answer the questions below. Attach the story you read to this worksheet.

1. What is the topic of this story? Is it relevant to readers of this publication?

   ____

2. Does the story have human interest? Explain.

   ____

   ____

   ____

3. Is the topic timely or timeless?

   ____

4. If it contains a news peg, identify the news peg.

   ____

5. How many sources are used? Name several, citing the particular paragraph(s) in which each appears.

   ____

   ____

   ____

6. Describe the format of the story. Does it have a clear beginning, middle, and end?

   ____

   ____

   ____

Name: ______________________________ Date: ______________

4.6 Analysis: Features (continued)

7. Describe the lead. Is it appropriate? effective? Why or why not?

____

____

8. What is the mood and tone of the feature? Use examples from the story to support your answer.

____

____

____

9. Does the story include incidents, anecdotes, and quotes? If so, note three of the most interesting and explain the idea or point that each illustrates.

____

____

____

____

10. How does the writer demonstrate creativity? Is the angle unusual? Does the writer show rather than tell? Use examples from the story to support your answer.

____

____

____

____

Name: ______________________________ Date: ______________

4.7 Types of Features

A. Match the types of features to their definitions by writing the correct letter on the blank next to the definition.

a. news feature

b. informative feature

c. personality profile

d. human-interest feature

e. historical feature

f. personal-accomplishment feature

g. shared-experience feature

h. how-to feature

____ 1. a story that explains how to do something

____ 2. a short piece (about 100 words), told in a unique or clever way, that concentrates on an unusual and emotionally appealing subject (person, place, object, or animal)

____ 3. a story that offers a human-interest view on a hard-news event

____ 4. a story about an interesting aspect of a historical subject, gathered from research and interviews

____ 5. a story that focuses on an individual who accomplished something amazing or who has overcome a particular life struggle

____ 6. a story that shares information gained from the writer's firsthand experience in doing something

____ 7. a story that reveals the personality of someone through incidents, anecdotes, and quotes (not through a list of accomplishments, favorite things, or biographical facts)

____ 8. a story that presents practical information on an interesting subject

B. Find examples of at least three different types of features. Label them and attach them to this worksheet.

Name: ______________________________ Date: ____________

4.8 Featurizing News

Look through a local or national newspaper. Read three hard-news stories covered in the publications you chose. Cite the publication, issue date, page number, and headline of each story. Then suggest at least two ideas for featurizing each hard-news report for your school newspaper. Where it seems a good idea, include ideas for sidebars or quick-read menus as well. Make sure your suggestions include ways to personalize and localize your featurized news stories.

Hard-news Story #1:

Publication: ______________________________ Issue date: __________

Headline: ______________________________ Page number: ________

Ideas for featurizing: ______________________________

____

Hard-news Story #2:

Publication: ______________________________ Issue date: __________

Headline: ______________________________ Page number: ________

Ideas for featurizing: ______________________________

____

Hard-news Story #3:

Publication: ______________________________ Issue date: __________

Headline: ______________________________ Page number: ________

Ideas for featurizing: ______________________________

____

Name: ______________________________ Date: ______________

4.9 Analysis: Sports

Read a newspaper sports story. Then answer the questions below. Attach the story you read to this worksheet.

1. What is (are) the sports event(s) covered in the story?

   ____

2. Would you define this story as a pregame story, a postgame story, or a mixture of both? Explain, using the criteria from pages 95 and 96 of the *Handbook.* Cite specific paragraphs in the story to support your answers.

   ____

   ____

   ____

   ____

   ____

   ____

3. Is the story featurized? Explain, drawing on examples from the story.

   ____

   ____

   ____

4. What is the story's angle?

   ____

   ____

   ____

Name: ____ Date: ________________

4.9 Analysis: Sports (continued)

5. Does the story use strong, active language and avoid clichés and jargon? Support your answer with examples from the story.

____

____

____

6. Does the story incorporate anecdotes and colorful quotes? If so, give an example.

____

____

7. If there is sports analysis or prediction in the story, is it supported with factual examples? Support your answer with examples from the story.

____

____

____

8. Is the coverage balanced? Explain, using examples from the story.

____

____

____

Name: ______________________________ Date: ______________

4.10 Action Writing

A. Read the sports story below. Circle the words and phrases that make this story say "Action!"

U.S. women's scoring spree figures to continue

Netherlands' top keeper unavailable for Sunday's match

by Bonnie DeSimone, Tribune Staff Writer

A second-string goalkeeper will play for the Netherlands against the U.S. women's soccer team at Soldier Field on Sunday.

Dutch starter Marleen Wissink, who came under heavy fire in a 5-0 U.S. win in Milwaukee on Thursday, has returned to Germany to play an important match for her club team.

That could mean even more of a score-fest for the United States, which has hammered 21 goals into rival nets in the last three games against relatively weak opponents.

It could be an episode of road rage on the Road to Pasadena tour leading up to the World Cup—so-called because the final, which the U.S. team fervently hopes to reach, will be played at the Rose Bowl. The outburst followed last month's dispiriting 2-1 loss to an increasingly dangerous-looking Chinese team, which scored the game-winner in extra time.

The defeat ended a 50-game win streak on U.S. soil.

"We have a bit of improvement to make, but we're closing the gap between where we are and where our best soccer is," coach Tony DeCicco said Friday in Chicago.

The most closely watched feet on the team belong to forward Mia Hamm, who needs two goals to break the all-time international scoring record held by retired Italian striker Elisabetta Vignotto.

Hamm endured an atypical eight-match scoring drought before notching goal No. 105 against Japan last month. She struck again Thursday against the Netherlands. Her most recent two-goal match was in last September's U.S. Cup against Russia.

The 1 p.m. match, which will be shown on ESPN2, also will serve as a dry run of sorts for Chicago's World Cup venue staff, which is expecting a crowd of about 30,000 if the weather is good.

About 47,000 tickets have been snapped up for the June 24 World Cup double-header that includes the U.S.-Nigeria game preceded by Brazil-Italy, and close to 30,000 for the June 26 twin-bill of Sweden-Ghana and defending champion Norway against Japan.

(From the *Chicago Tribune,* May 16, 1999, Chicago, IL)

Name: ______________________________ Date: ______________

4.10 Action Writing (continued)

B. Rewrite the sentences below to make them more active. You may also need to make them more clear, concise, and colorful. Feel free to break up a long sentence into two shorter sentences.

1. The muddy field caused the rugby players to fall down a lot.

____

____

2. Jim McHale, 8th grade, took the ball up the court and made an outside shot, which put the team ahead by two points.

____

____

3. The rock climbers who qualified for the Scramblers Club, which included Jade Kava and Tina Singh, 9th grade, had to go all the way to the top of an 85-foot cliff.

____

____

4. The hockey team keeps in shape by doing in-line skating during the summer.

____

____

5. Juan Costina, 6th grade, overturned his canoe when he tried to stand in it.

____

____

Name: ______________________________ Date: ______________

4.11 Covering Sports

Attend a sports event. It may be a team or nonteam event. It may be a school sport or a recreational sport. If you're unfamiliar with the sport and the players, do some research first. Write up your coverage as a sports short below. You may set it up like a news brief or in an outline format, as shown on page 98 of the *Handbook.*

If you have permission from your sports editor to cover the event for an upcoming issue, you should also talk to various sources. As you write your story, follow the guidelines for writing winning sports stories and for maintaining objectivity. Attach your finished draft of the story to this worksheet.

Name: ______________________________ Date: ______________

4.12 Sports Features

Working with a partner or a small group, brainstorm sports and recreation topics for possible running features or single-focus features. For running features, you might brainstorm topics for different types of personality profiles, shared-experience features, informative features, and how-to features. For single-focus features, brainstorm topics for each of the four seasons. Write your ideas below in the form of a web.

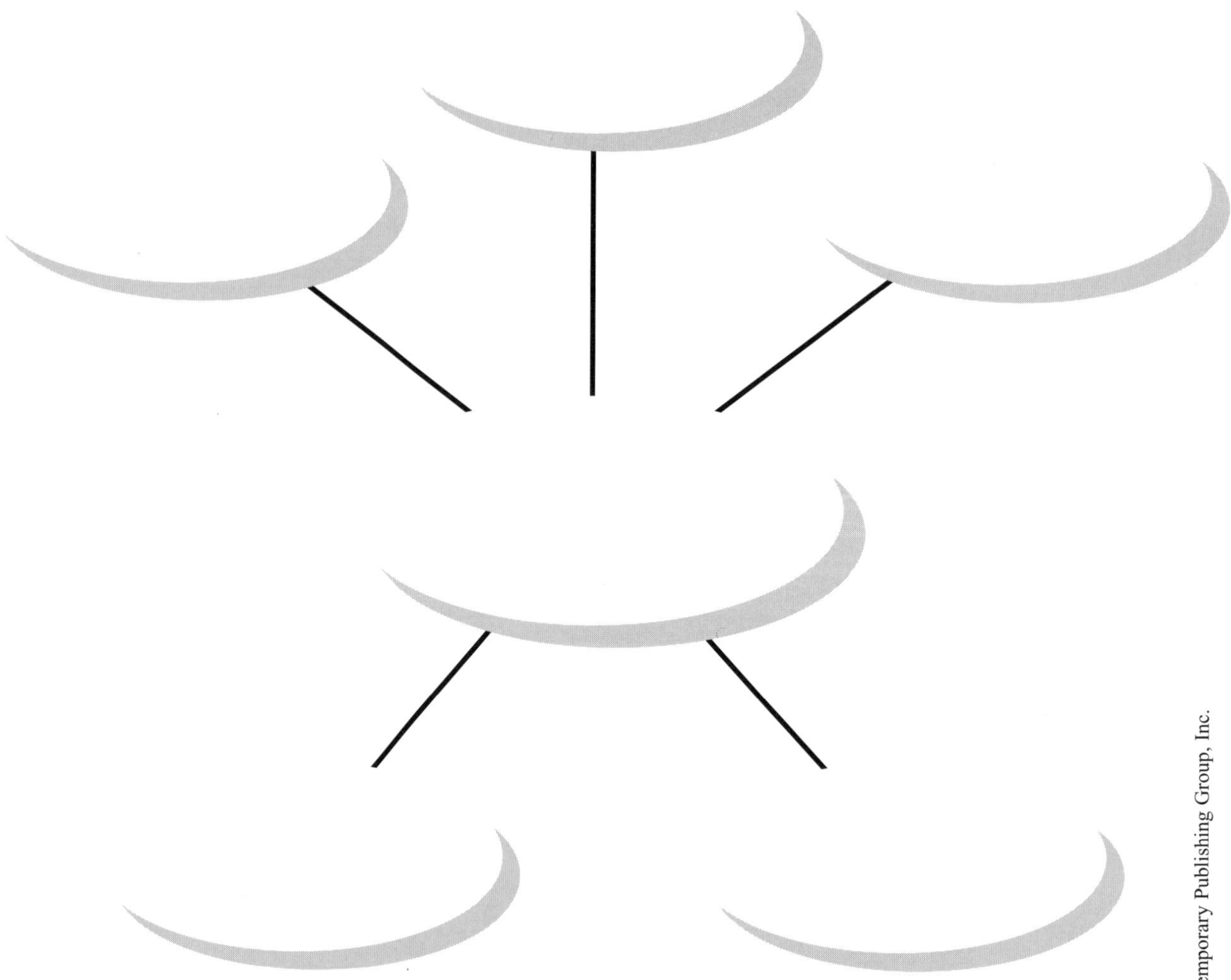

Name: ____________________ Date: __________

4.13 Analysis: Editorials

Read a newspaper editorial (not a column or a review). Then answer the questions below. Attach the editorial you read to this worksheet.

1. What is the topic of this editorial?

___

2. What news elements does this topic possess?

___

3. Is the topic localized? If so, how?

___

___

4. What opinion does the editorial state about the topic?

___

___

5. Are all opinions supported with facts, examples, or expert opinions? Support your answer with an example from the editorial.

___

___

6. Does the editorial follow the general structure for editorials? Explain.

___

___

Name: ______________________________ Date: ______________

4.13 Analysis: Editorials (continued)

7. What is the purpose, or function, of the editorial?

____

8. Does the editorial follow the organization for this type of editorial? Explain, using examples from the editorial.

____

____

____

____

9. Does the editorial appear to be balanced and well researched? Support your answer with an example from the editorial.

____

____

10. Does the writer make the point clearly and get to it quickly?

____

11. If the editorial suggests a solution, is it logical and practical? Explain your answer.

____

____

12. Does the conclusion leave you with a clear understanding of the writer's opinion? Does it stimulate you to think and feel?

____

Name: ______________________________ Date: ______________

4.14 Functions of Editorials

Read the editorial below. Then answer the questions that follow. (Note that although this editorial is signed, it doesn't use the personal pronoun *I* and so likely expresses the official opinion of the newspaper.)

No bee? How can this be?

by Spencer Maki

How do you spell *uninvited?*

Southeast Missouri spellers are not invited to the *St. Louis Post-Dispatch* Regional Spelling Bee this year. The outlying regions of the state have been cut from participating in this annual *Post-Dispatch* spelling competition.

For over 20 years, the *Post* has sponsored the regional bee for district spelling champions all around the region. But due to budget restrictions and growth of interest in the bee, the newspaper has cut all but the St. Louis metropolitan schools from its funding for this year.

A spokesperson at the *Post,* public relations department manager Tracy Rouch, said the paper plans to completely discontinue sponsorship of the bee after this year.

During the past 20 years, spellers from around the state have competed in local school bees, with school winners moving on to district round, and the winners there moving on to the St. Louis contest in February or March.

The St. Louis regional champion then has advanced on to the Scripps-Howard National Spelling Bee in Washington, D.C. The National Bee is in its 73rd year and is a tradition which is expected to draw over 10 million contestants at the local level in 1998.

This decision by the *Post-Dispatch* leaves a large part of the state without a sponsor for this year's bee. Spellers in southeast Missouri will have no place to go after school rounds.

Teachers who have worked with this program in the past are having trouble understanding how the *Post-Dispatch* could think of dropping this long-standing bee at the very time interest is increasing.

For Missouri students who have no bee to enter this year, the decision is spelled b-a-d.

(From *The Paw,* December 19, 1997, Schultz Middle School, Cape Girardeau, MO)

1. What is (are) the function(s) of this editorial?

____

2. Does it follow the organization for this type of editorial?

____

Name: ______________________ Date: ____________

4.15 Writing an Editorial

On the lines below, write an editorial on a topic of your choice. Make sure you evaluate your topic first, using the questions on page 104 of the *Handbook*. You may wish to submit your editorial to your editorial board to consider for an upcoming issue.

Name: ______________________________ Date: ______________

4.16 Sampling: Editorial Cartoons

In the space below, attach an editorial cartoon that you think is especially effective. Under the cartoon, write what you think the cartoon means and why you think it's effective. Be prepared to discuss your chosen cartoon with others in class.

Name: ______________________________ Date: ______________

4.17 Drawing an Editorial Cartoon

In the space below, draw an editorial cartoon. Your cartoon may or may not have a news peg, but it should be relevant to the readers of your school newspaper.

Follow the tips for drawing editorial cartoons on page 113 of the *Handbook.* If you aren't skilled at drawing, you may just sketch your idea using stick figures. You may also describe how you would have the idea represented more completely by another student who is more skilled at drawing.

Name: ______________________________ Date: ______________

4.18 Analysis: Columns

Read a newspaper or magazine column. Then answer the questions below. Attach the column you read to this worksheet.

1. What is the topic of this column?

   ____

2. What angle does the writer take on the topic?

   ____

3. Is the topic localized? If so, how?

   ____

4. What opinion does the writer express about the topic?

   ____

   ____

5. Is the opinion stated up front or revealed further into the column?

   ____

6. Does the writer use examples and anecdotes to illustrate his or her points? Support your answer with an example from the column.

   ____

   ____

7. Does the writer credit sources that helped form his or her opinions? If so, give an example from the column.

   ____

8. Is the style the writer uses in sync with the column's angle and tone?

   ____

Name: ______________________________ Date: ______________

4.19 Sampling: Columns

Find a column that you think is especially well done. Attach it to this worksheet. On the lines below, write why you think it's effective. Be prepared to discuss your chosen column with others in class.

Name: ______________________ Date: ____________

4.20 Analysis: Reviews

Read a newspaper or magazine review. Then answer the questions below. Attach the review you read to this worksheet.

1. What is the product or performance covered in this review?

____

2. How does the writer review the product or performance? Check those that apply.

   - ☐ itemizes the strengths and weaknesses of the product or performance
   - ☐ compares and contrasts the product or performance with another of the same type
   - ☐ evaluates the product or performance on the basis of how well it fulfills its intended purpose

3. Does the review concentrate on meaningful characteristics of the product or performance? Support your answer with an example from the review.

____

4. What is the overall opinion of the writer about the product or performance?

____

5. Does the reviewer support his or her opinions with specific examples? Support your answer with an example from the review.

____

6. Is the review more than just a ratings device?

____

7. Is the review timely?

____

8. Does the review serve the readers? Explain your answer.

____

Name: ______________________ Date: ____________

4.21 Sampling: Reviews

Find a review that you think is especially well done. Attach it to this worksheet. On the lines below, write why you think it's effective. Be prepared to discuss your chosen review with others in class.

Name: ______________________________ Date: ____________

5.1 Copyfitting

A. Read the following paragraphs and edit each to 35 words or less. Follow your school's stylebook as you edit. Or use the stylebook on page 245 of the *Handbook* if you don't have one. Keep an eye out for editorializing.

1. The school board also voted to build a new addition to the school library. Principal Glen Burris pointed to the problem repeatedly during recent school board meetings. He stressed that there is not enough room in the current library to hold all the books and the new computer lab.

____

____

____

____

2. The Drama Club is actively searching for new members to join their club. They are looking for people who enjoy theatre and working with others. Anyone that is interested is encouraged to come to the next meeting of the Drama Club on October 8. At the meeting, new members will be introduced to the Drama Club's current members, its officers, and its purpose.

____

____

____

B. Imagine that you need to fill more space for a short story announcing the election of new student council officers. What could you do?

____

____

____

Name: ______________________________ Date: ______________

5.2 Copyediting Tools and Resources

Match the copyediting tool or resource to the copyediting task by writing the correct letter on the blank next to the description of the task. Use each term only once.

a. stylebook

b. spell checker

c. dictionary

d. thesaurus

e. grammar handbook

f. telephone book

g. school directory or homeroom list

h. almanac

i. CD-ROM encyclopedia

____ 1. You're trying to find something to replace the word *fast.*

____ 2. You're looking for the singular form of the word *data.*

____ 3. You're looking for the exact date on which a recent political event took place.

____ 4. The library is closed, but the computer room is open. You need to verify a fact about hang gliding.

____ 5. You need to verify the correct spelling of a local department store's name.

____ 6. You need to verify the spelling of a teacher's name.

____ 7. You need to find out how your school newspaper handles film titles.

____ 8. You're about to print out the final version of the edited story. You have one more word-processing step to perform.

____ 9. You're a bit confused on the proper use of the semicolon.

Name: ______________________________ Date: ______________

5.3 Copyediting Practice

A. Copyedit the following sentences. Use your stylebook or the stylebook provided on page 245 of the *Handbook*. Use the standard copyediting symbols. Make your marks in red pencil or pen.

1. Most of the members of the coed track team are male but three are female.
2. Mrs. Leanne Honeywell's seventh grade homeroom is publishing a pet calendar.
3. The cops say students should be on lookout for the suspect adn should call the police if you see anything suspicious.
4. Try-outs for the Spring musical are going to be held in the auditorium from 3 o'clock to 5 o'clock on the evening of May 3.
5. Mr. Finn told the history class that on May 10 they would be attending a field trip to Chicago's Museum of Natural History.
6. On January 7, the gymnasium walls were painted an ugly shade of green.
7. The suspect had been hanging around in front of the convenience store for a long time, according to witnesses.
8. Eating too many sweets makes people fat.
9. "Your muscles must be warm when you stretch" stated athletic trainer Joy Blue.
10. Principal Quinn has always been fair to one and all.

Name: ______________________________ Date: ______________

5.3 Copyediting Practice (continued)

B. Copyedit the editorial below. Use your stylebook or the stylebook provided on page 245 of the *Handbook*. Use the standard copyediting symbols. Make your marks in red pencil or pen.

KG.99.3.LOCKER EDITORIAL
3/10/99

There have been a rash of theifs at our school recently. It wouldn't be so bad if students were just leaving their belongings around out of pure carelessness. But htat isn't the case .The theif (or theifs), have been breaking into peoples' lockers. Yes, that's right: lockers. A student' s 1 safe haven. A place where personal posessions can be kept under lck and key. A place where only one person knows the combination, right?

Wrong.

Someone or several someone's have the combination to to at least 5 seperate lockers. Because those five lockers have been ripped off in the past couple o fmonths. The theifts usually take place btween during first and 3rd period. So how do we catch these people. Well, one thing you can do is to not give out your locker combination to ANYone. If you do, you deserve whatever you get. Seriously. Also a good idea is anyone who has infromation about the locker theifs should get in touch with Principle Stuart. She will make sure your name is anonymous. Lets all work together to solve thiis ever growing problem,

Name: ______________________________ Date: ______________

5.4 Proofreading Practice

Below is a copyedited story. Proofread the corrected proof on the next page to make sure all corrections have been made. Follow the directions for reading and marking on page 131 of the *Handbook*. Make your marks in red pencil or pen.

M.P.00.2.COYOTE

2/12/00

by Maria Paloma

"I though maybe I was still asleep," said runner Jim Reyes, 9th grade. "Then I thought may be it was a dog." What he and other track team members saw crossing their path during an early morning run September 19 was probably a coyote, ~~according to~~ Kris Amendala of the Mount Doe Animal Control Unit.

You'd be surprised how many wild animals are around," said Amandela. "Besides coyotes, there are possums, coons, porcupines, and foxes." ~~That's a lot of animals roaming around!~~ She explained that the animals are ~~pretty much~~ driven out of thier natural habitate by new housing developments and come into the city looking for food.

Will the coyote survive in the city? "Hard to tell," said Amendala. "Depends on whether it escapes freeway traffic and can find enough to eat." What if it is caught? "~~Oh,~~ we'll take it outside city limits," said Amendala.

"I thought it was the Carson team mascot sent to spy on us!" said Track Coach Sam Adolfson. "They're the coyotes, after all.

-end-

Name: ____________________ Date: __________

5.4 Proofreading Practice (continued)

M.P.00.2.COYOTE

2/12/00

by Maria Paloma

"I thought maybe I was still asleep," said runner Jim Reyes, 8th grade. "Then I thought maybe it was a dog."

What Reyes and other track team members saw crossing their path during an early morning run Sept. 19 was probably a coyote, said Kris Amendala of the Mount Doe Animal Control Unit.

You'd be surprised how many wild animals are around," said Amendala. "Besides coyotes, there are possums, raccoons, porcupines, and foxes." She explained that the animals are driven out of their natural habitats by new housing developments and come into the city looking for food.

Will the coyote survive in the city? "Hard to tell," said Amendala. "That depends on whether it escapes freeway traffic and can find enough to eat." What if it is caught? "we'll take it outside city limits," said Amendala.

"I thought it was the Carson team mascot sent to spy on us!" said assistant track coach Sam Adolfson. "They're the Coyotes, after all.

-end-

Name: ______________________________ Date: ____________

6.1 Goals of Newspaper Design

Working with a partner, evaluate your newspaper or another newspaper to determine whether it fulfills the three goals of newspaper design:

1. It must invite the reader into the paper with an attractive visual presentation.
2. It must lead the reader in an orderly way through the paper, drawing attention to content, pointing out its relative importance, and highlighting which content is related.
3. It must assist the reader by making all content readable.

Write your evaluation on the lines below. Support your opinions with references to specific examples. Attach the newspaper you evaluated to this worksheet.

Name: ______________________________ Date: ______________

6.2 Design Principles

The six principles of design are unity, consistency, dominance, contrast, repetition, and balance. Find a well-designed newspaper. On the lines below, describe how the newspaper's design exhibits each of these principles. Give at least one example for each principle. Refer to page 136 in the *Handbook* to review each term. Attach the newspaper you reviewed to this worksheet.

Unity:

____

____

Consistency:

____

____

Dominance:

____

____

Contrast:

____

____

Repetition:

____

____

Balance:

____

____

Name: ______________________ Date: __________

6.3 Page Elements

Choose the term that matches the definition by writing the letter on the blank next to the definition.

___ 1. a headline for a regular item in each issue of a newspaper

a. subhead c. standing head

b. masthead d. jumphead

___ 2. copy that lists page numbers on which each section starts

a. folio c. teaser

b. index d. refer

___ 3. an identification mark, usually consisting of copy combined with a graphic

a. infographic c. icon

b. logo d. bullet

___ 4. a shaded area, measured in percentages

a. bleed c. spread

b. overprint d. screen

___ 5. white space that separates columns and facing pages

a. external margin c. rule

b. guttcr d. doublc-truck

Name: ______________________________ Date: ______________

6.4 Thumbnails and Dummies

A. In the boxes below, create thumbnails for three pages of a recent school or local paper.

B. When you have completed your three thumbnails, use a grid paper to create a dummy for one of the pages. Follow the tips on pages 144–145 of the *Handbook.* With permission from your teacher, you may create your grid and your dummy using desktop publishing software.

Name: ______________________________ Date: ______________

6.5 Typography Terms

Match the typography terms to their definitions by writing the correct letter on the blank next to the definition. Use each term only once.

a. typography
b. character
c. typeface
d. font
e. family
f. weight
g. width
h. posture
i. leading
j. letterspacing
k. reverse print
l. serif
m. sans serif
n. script
o. novelty

___ 1. space between letters in a line of copy
___ 2. fonts closely related in style
___ 3. a class of type that reflects a particular mood or historic period
___ 4. a design of a complete set of type characters, specified by a name
___ 5. a class of type that resembles handwriting
___ 6. the slant of a letter
___ 7. the horizontal measure of a type character
___ 8. a type letter or letterform
___ 9. a class of type without serifs
___ 10. the space between the baseline of one line of type and the baseline of the next, measured in points
___ 11. a class of type with small "feet" or strokes at the ends of most letters
___ 12. a complete set of characters in one size and style of a typeface
___ 13. the visual width of the strokes that make up each letter
___ 14. light type on a dark background
___ 15. the way printed letters are handled on a page

Name: ______________________________ Date: ______________

6.6 Sampling: Typography

Find an example of typography that you think is especially well done. Attach it to this worksheet. On the lines below, write why you think it's effective. Be prepared to discuss your chosen type treatment with others in class.

Name: ______________________ Date: ____________

6.7 Analysis: Graphics

Using your own newspaper or another, answer the questions below. Attach the newspaper you analyzed to this worksheet.

1. What types of graphics are used in this paper?

   ____

2. Do the graphics that are used to emphasize and distinguish page elements serve their function well? In particular, do they follow the guidelines described on page 160 of the *Handbook?* Explain, citing examples from the newspaper.

   ____

   ____

   ____

3. Do the photographs and other graphics serve the communication function well? Support your opinion with examples from the newspaper.

   ____

   ____

4. When graphics are used to clarify a concept, are they effective? Why or why not? Give one specific example.

   ____

   ____

5. How do the graphics in this newspaper serve to unify the design and create a visual identity for the paper? Support your answer with examples.

   ____

   ____

   ____

Name: ______________________________ Date: ______________

6.8 Infographics

Create an infographic using one of the three sets of data provided below. Make sure it follows the rules for infographics outlined on page 161 of the *Handbook.* You may draw your infographic (neatly!) or complete it using desktop publishing software. Attach your infographic to this worksheet.

Data Set #1: Results from a poll of 50 students who were asked, "What's your #1 favorite pizza topping?"

- pepperoni: 20 (40%); extra cheese: 10 (20%); sausage: 8 (16%); other: 7 (14%); mushrooms: 5 (10%)

Data Set #2: Based on information from Jansport, a backpack company, on the amount of weight someone should carry in a student backpack, or book bag, (10–15 percent of body weight)

- weight/backpack weight: 100 lbs./10–15 lbs.; 120 lbs./12–18 lbs.; 140 lbs./14–21 lbs.; 160 lbs./16–24 lbs.; 180 lbs./18–27 lbs.; 200 lbs./20–30 lbs.

Data Set #3: A basic setup for a home video shoot

- light-colored, plain backdrop behind talent (people performing); backdrop should extend at least three feet on either side of acting area of talent
- two lights, one positioned on each side of backdrop and angled in toward it
- a video camera, at least five feet in front of talent to allow a comfortable acting area; camera should be on tripod and be able to swivel to view entire acting area

Name: ______________________________ Date: ______________

6.9 Analysis: Display Ad

Find a newspaper display ad that you think is well done. Attach the ad to this worksheet. Label the elements of the display ad, including the pitch, close, and slogan (if any). On the lines below, explain why you think the ad is effective.

____

____

____

Name: ______________________________ Date: ____________

6.10 Designing a Display Ad

Create a display ad, following the specs provided below. Make sure it follows the guidelines for ads with impact on page 161. Create thumbnails first. Then make a dummy of your display ad or complete it using desktop publishing software. Attach your ad to this worksheet.

Specs #1: 1/4 page ad for Preston Hardware

- *Benefit heads:* Here comes Homecoming! 10% off float supplies for Tiger fans!
- *Pitch:* Shop Preston Hardware for all your float-building supplies. We carry chicken wire, napkins, paint, brushes, spray paint, foamcore, wood, nails, hammers, glue, staple guns, posterboard, markers, and streamers.
- *Close:* For the best selection, come in today!
- *Slogan:* Serving the community since 1889
- *Graphic:* a Homecoming float with the caption "Go Tigers!" or illustrations of some of the supplies mentioned
- *Identification:* Preston Hardware, 223 Wilson Blvd., Tama, NY (213) 555-1633

Name: ______________________________ Date: ______________

6.11 Paste-up

Imagine you've been assigned to design a feature page for your student newspaper containing the page elements as defined below.

First create thumbnails (in the space provided on the next page). Then create a dummy of the thumbnail you like best (on a grid sheet). Finally, create a completed paste-up of the page, using dark gray boxes for photos, white boxes for ads, and nonsense copy or screened boxes for stories. Attach your dummy and completed paste-up to this worksheet.

As you prepare your layout and paste-up, follow the guidelines for standout layout described on pages 147–149 of the *Handbook* as well as the guidelines for placing ads on page 167. You might want to use modular design, as described on page 146.

- first-dating expectations story (9–10 column inches)
- headline and byline for dating story
- pull quote in dating story
- quick-read menu on dating taboos (3–5 column inches)
- headline for quick-read menu
- graphic for dating story or quick-read menu
- random-opinion poll (4 photos of students, with quote for each)
- ad for movie theater (9 column inches)
- ad for restaurant (20 column inches)
- ad for restaurant (12 column inches)
- section head (features)
- folio

Name: ______________________________ Date: ______________

6.11 Paste-up (continued)

Draw your thumbnails for your feature page in the space below. Make them about the same dimensions as your newspaper's format.

Name: ______________________________ Date: ______________

7.1 Photo Assignments

With another student, brainstorm the types of photos that might be assigned for each of the stories described below. Note the functions each photo might serve: communication, credibility, visual appeal, and vitality.

1. an advance story on regional marching band competitions, which will be held at your school

   ____

   ____

2. a coverage story on two students who were lost overnight in a nearby forest preserve

   ____

   ____

3. a coverage story on problems associated with the student use of pagers and cell phones during school hours

   ____

   ____

4. a follow-up story on rusting lockers in the locker rooms, focusing on the inadequate repair rather than replacement

   ____

   ____

5. an advance story on a school-sponsored arts festival showcasing student sculpture, paintings, crafts, theatre, and videos

   ____

   ____

Name: ______________________________ Date: ______________

7.2 Role-play: Photo Shoot

With two other students, role-play a photo shoot, based on the information in the photo assignment form below.

One student should portray the photographer, another the subject of the photograph, and the third the reporter or another subject. The photographer should gather the cutline information. Be sure to consider whether you need a photo release for your shoot.

Don't script the role-play. Instead, improvise the situation to better simulate the kinds of surprises and challenges faced during a shoot.

On the lines below, evaluate the effectiveness of your shoot.

Name: ______________________________ Date: ______________

7.3 Parts of a Camera

In the word-search puzzle, circle each of the camera parts defined below. The terms appear horizontally, vertically, and diagonally. No terms appear backwards.

1. the light-tight box that houses the camera parts
2. the part of the camera through which the light enters, is sharpened, and is transmitted to the film or solar cell
3. a device that slides back and forth to control the amount of time the film or solar cell is exposed to light
4. a mechanism to release the shutter
5. the lens opening that controls how much light gets through the shutter
6. a framing device that allows the photographer to see the picture before it's taken
7. indicates the aperture (lens opening) in numbers
8. indicates the depth of field when the camera is focused on a subject at a particular f-stop
9. indicates how fast the shutter opens and closes, measured in fractions of a second

J S P E R T O O H U T T M O I S Q V K I

S H U T T E R D M E R F Y Z L O B N G R

D U D L O O K R T H I E S S L P T O Z Y

A T P E L M S H R K H I L H O M R A D L

R T E E P O R S C T F L H U N Q Z H U Y

P E W N A T E U L R S O C T E R S P E E

S R D I P J H X J O K L I T Z X T C O L

B R L E E K R O T A P R E E R N F R O U

C E P L R Q N S F I E L W R I E S A F T

T L T X S I R J V F M R T S C J T Y R T

A E H I H O F U S P I J A P U R O Z E D

Q A P E R T U R E M S E L E J I P I O X

V S H U C K S P L A K L L E C Z O L F R

W E L T I N F I E L E N K D U P R S R E

L U D S E O O Z H E N U F E S H U T T P

P A J L E E S P I N T O S I R C S R E M

S T T Q I Z K I F R E M K C S R A T H I

E U V I E W F I N D E R O D E P T L E W

K I L P X L E N Z T T E R O L I T Y E E

Name: ______________________________ Date: ____________

7.4 Lenses

Write the type of lens you would use in each of the following situations and why:

1. You're at the Grand Canyon, and you want your photograph to show as much of the canyon as possible.

____

____

2. You want a shot of a deer grazing on the edge of the school's soccer field 200 yards away.

____

____

____

3. You're shooting the finals of the 400-yard dash. You're at the finish line when you see the runner from your school edging ahead at the far turn on the other side of the track. You want to get a shot of her in the lead.

____

____

4. You're shooting a portrait of a teacher, sitting in his fishing boat on the pond behind his house. The setting is very scenic. You're on the dock a few yards away.

____

____

____

5. You're shooting a large group of people at fairly close range.

____

____

Name: ______________________________ Date: ______________

7.5 Exposure and Focus

A. Look at the photograph below and answer the questions that follow.

PHOTO BY BECKY BUTTERFIELD

1. Was the film speed the photographer used probably relatively fast or slow? Explain your answer.

 ____

2. Was the shutter speed the photographer used most likely relatively fast or slow? Explain your answer.

 ____

3. What if more light was needed? What could the photographer do and how might it affect the photograph? Explain your answer.

 ____

 ____

 ____

Name: ______________________________ Date: ______________

7.5 Exposure and Focus (continued)

B. Look at the photograph below. On the lines provided, explain the function of the photo and how the depth of field used enhances the photo and its function(s).

PHOTO BY JENNIFER KRAMER

____

____

____

____

____

____

____

____

Name: ______________________________ Date: ______________

7.6 Lighting

Look at the photograph below and answer the questions that follow.

PHOTO BY ANDY JACKSON

1. What is the light direction used? What seems to be the light source?

____

2. Where was the photographer positioned in the theatre to get this shot?

____

3. How does the lighting affect the subject and the artistic quality of the photograph?

____

____

____

4. What mood is created by the lighting of this photo?

____

5. Do you think the photographer used a flash for this photo? Explain your answer.

____

____

Name: ______________________________________ Date: _____________

7.7 Sampling: Lighting

Find a photograph in a newspaper that uses light effectively. Attach it to this worksheet. On the lines below, write why you think the lighting is effective. Explain any use of directional lighting and comment on the quality of light in the photo you chose. Be prepared to discuss the photo with others in class.

Name: ______________________________ Date: ______________

7.8 Composition

What composition techniques were used in this photograph? Evaluate the photo on the lines below. Support your opinions with specific points about the photo.

PHOTO BY NICK KENIG

Name: ______________________________ Date: ______________

7.9 Sampling: Composition

Find a photograph in a newspaper that exhibits good composition. Attach it to this worksheet. On the lines below, write what composition techniques were used and why you think the composition is effective. Be prepared to discuss the photo with others in class.

Name: ______________________________ Date: ______________

7.10 Cropping

A. How would you crop this action photo to make it stronger? Use two L-shaped pieces of cardboard to define the cropped area. Make crop marks to show where you would crop it. Make sure you follow the guidelines on pages 200–201 of the *Handbook.* On the lines below, explain why you cropped it as you did.

PHOTO BY MELISSA DROSJACK

Name: ______________________________ Date: ______________

7.10 Cropping (continued)

B. Find a photograph in a newspaper that you feel would benefit from cropping. Use two L-shaped pieces of cardboard to define the cropped area. Make crop marks on it and attach it to this worksheet. On the lines below, explain why you cropped it as you did.

____

____

____

____

____

Name: ______________________________ Date: ______________

8.1 Evaluating the Budget

A. Ask your business manager to examine the records for a specific issue of the paper or for one month to determine the various sources of income for your school paper. List amounts in the categories below.

Advertising:

____

Subscriptions:

____

School subsidies:

____

Direct sales:

____

Contributors:

____

Grants:

____

Civic clubs:

____

Parent-teacher associations:

____

Printer:

____

Fund-raisers:

____

Staff-parent garage sales:

____

Vending boxes:

____

Other:

____

8.1 Evaluating the Budget (continued)

B. Now do the same to determine the various expenses for your school paper. List amounts in the categories below.

Production Costs:

____

____

____

____

Distribution Costs:

____

____

____

____

Miscellaneous Costs:

____

____

____

____

C. Add all of the income sources together. Then add all of the expenses together. Subtract the expenses from the income. This is the profit for the period. If the expenses total is greater than the income total, show the deficit, or losses. Write the profit or deficit here:

____

Name: ______________________ Date: ____________

8.2 Record Keeping

A. Get into practice for daily newspaper record keeping by keeping a record of your personal financial transactions (income and expenses) for one week. Use the daily account ledger form provided below (or one of your own forms). Keep your receipts to confirm your expenses. Begin with your current balance (the amount of money you have at the beginning of the week's records). Each day, compute your daily balance, double-checking your calculations.

If you use one of your own forms, or an electronic accounting program, attach your ledger for the week to this worksheet.

Daily Account Ledger Form

Date	Description	Income	Expense	Balance

Name: ______________________________ Date: ______________

8.2 Record Keeping (continued)

B. Practice transferring information from a daily account into running accounts, using the information provided below.

Daily Account Ledger Form

Date	Description	Income	Expense	Balance
4/18/00	film (Ray's Drugstore)		12.28	828.40
4/18/00	$Mart (prepaid 4" ad)	24.00		852.40
4/19/00	red pens (Ray's Drugstore)		15.03	837.37
4/21/00	direct sales	71.00		908.37
4/24/00	postage		38.33	870.04
4/26/00	Paul Crace (subscr.)	15.00		885.04

Accounts Payable Form

Place of Purchase	Date of Purchase	Date Billed	Amount Spent	Description of Purchase	Date Paid	Amount Paid

Name: ____________________ Date: ____________

8.3 Charting the Ad-Sales Process

Draw a flowchart of your newspaper's ad-sales process. Make sure it's clear what is happening at each stage. Take special care to show which actions happen at the same time and which happen in a particular sequence.

Name: ______________________________ Date: ______________

8.4 Computing Advertising Income

Using the information provided below, compute the amount of advertising your paper needs to sell for this issue. Follow the steps on page 212 of the *Handbook,* which are repeated here. Show your work next to each step.

Expenses: $650

Income other than advertising: $335

Column inches of ads sold, at $5 column inch: 25

1. Subtract the total income *other than advertising* projected for the issue from the total expenses projected for the issue.
2. Check the advertiser contracts to see which advertisers have bought ads to run in the issue. Total up the income as well as the column inches for those ads.
3. Subtract the income of the sold ads from your previous total in Step 1. This is the advertising income needed for the issue.
4. Divide the total from step 3 by the cost of a column inch, according to your rate sheet. This is the number of column inches you need to sell.
5. Add the column inches from Step 2 and Step 4. This is how many column inches you need to leave space for in the pages.

Name: ______________________________ Date: ______________

8.5 Market Research

Working in pairs, conduct market research on teen spending habits by looking at advertisements in media aimed at teenagers (including the Internet). Make a list of the types of products advertised to teenagers. Use this information and the yellow pages to find businesses in your area that sell these types of products. Write a summary of your findings below. Explain how you might use what you learned to sell advertising space in your newspaper to these businesses.

Name: ______________________________ Date: ______________

8.6 Scripting a Sales Presentation

Script a sales presentation that incorporates all the elements described on page 216 of the *Handbook.* Study the script and practice it until it sounds completely natural. Perform your presentation for your classmates.

Greeting:

____

____

Sales pitch:

____

____

____

____

____

____

Close:

____

____

____

Wrap-up:

____

____

____

Name: ______________________________ Date: ______________

8.7 Distribution Methods

A. Draw a chart that shows your newspaper's readership and distribution methods for each group of readers (see page 220 of the *Handbook).*

Name: ______________________ Date: ____________

8.7 Distribution Methods (continued)

B. In a small group, discuss any possible problems with your paper's distribution methods. What better or additional methods might be used? How can you maintain or expand readership with these methods? Write your ideas below.

Name: ______________________ Date: __________

9.1 Freedom of the Press

Imagine that you are the editor-in-chief of your school newspaper. Think about each of the issues described below and explain what decision you would make and why. Before doing so, review any policies or guidelines of your newspaper.

1. One of your reporters has written an editorial that claims that students have a constitutional right to wear team jackets and other sports-related clothing from NBA or NFL teams. In the past, such clothing has been a source of gang violence on school grounds. Do you run the editorial? Why or why not?

____

____

____

____

2. Some students have started wearing T-shirts printed with racist or sexist slogans. What's the newspaper's official position on this issue?

____

____

____

____

Name: ________________________________ Date:______________

9.1 Freedom of the Press (continued)

3. One of your top reporters has written an article that includes an anecdote based on a rumor about a deeply embarrassing incident in a faculty member's personal life. Almost everyone knows the rumor is true. The faculty member has not denied it. Do you print the story?

4. A contributing artist to your paper has created an illustration of Bambi (from the Disney movie) for an article on hunting. It's obviously the Disney character. The art came in late, almost missing the final deadline. The rest of the page is already pasted-up. You have reserved space for the art. What do you do?

5. Your principal hears that you're running an editorial critical of a new truancy policy. The principal wants to see the editorial before it's printed, "just to make sure the facts are correct." Do you let your principal see it?

Name: ______________________________ Date: ______________

9.2 Freedom of Expression

For each example below and on the next page, one of the following terms applies. On the blank lines, write the word or phrase that best describes the example. Not every term is used.

copyright violation	libel	provable truth
fair-comment rule	obscenity	public figure
fighting words	prior review	public official
invasion of privacy	privilege	slander

1. Your school newspaper printed some very inflammatory comments about a power plant down the street from the school grounds. The comments were based on stated facts. If you are sued for libel, you can defend yourself in court with ______________________.

2. The power plant later went to court. The school newspaper followed the court proceedings closely and printed monthly updates. The information the paper used is immune from libel under the defense of ______________________.

3. At a school board meeting, one of the reporters from the school paper makes an untrue negative comment about the board president. This reporter is guilty of ______________.

4. A student submits an editorial that turns out to have been written by a well-known author. The student uses his own name in the byline, which constitutes ______________________.

5. An anonymous student turns in an editorial cartoon that contains ethnic slurs, which might constitute ______________________.

Name: ____________________________________ Date: ______________

9.2 Freedom of Expression (continued)

6. The school newspaper has printed a comment about the science teacher, claiming he has a prison record. The comment turns out to be false, making the paper guilty of ________________.

7. State law denies Gray Lake High School's principal the right to read the paper's lead story before it is printed. The state does not allow ________________________.

8. At Newton Middle School, a feature article about a mysterious elderly man living just down the street from the school grounds has just been scrapped. The editor-in-chief claimed the story might be seen as ______________________________.

9. The Muskegon Middle School *Plainspeaker* runs a short-story contest each year and prints the top three stories in a special edition. This year one of the stories contains adult language and sexually graphic situations. The author claims it is not ____________________ because of its artistic and literary value.

10. Last month the Blue Falls High School *Epic* ran a humorous column based on rumors about the wild nightlife of the governor. The editors aren't worried about this speculation because the governor is considered a ________________________.

Name: ______________________________ Date: ______________

9.3 Code of Ethics

In the space below, create a code of ethics for your school or local newspaper. Use as your model the categories shown on page 231 of the *Handbook,* but make the wording fit your specific point of view and purpose.

Name: ______________________________ Date: ______________

9.4 Being Sensitive

Part of a journalist's duty is to be sensitive to language that might be considered by certain groups to be offensive. Look at the pairs of terms below. Circle the more politically correct term.

1. deaf/hearing-impaired
2. persons with disabilities/handicapped people
3. old people/the elderly
4. police officer/cop
5. woman/lady
6. mentally disabled/retarded
7. mentally ill/crazy
8. black person/African American
9. slum/low-income housing
10. homeless person/street person

Name: ______________________________ Date: ______________

9.5 Taking Responsibility

Think about the following situations that might occur in the life of a reporter. On the blank lines, explain what you would most likely do in each situation.

1. You are writing a springtime feature on romance. You get a phoned-in tip from an anonymous caller who claims to have secretly winessed the surprise engagement of two teachers at an area resort. When you press the caller for his name, he hangs up. You are one hour from deadline. What do you do with this information?

____

____

____

2. One of the people you interview for your feature on coaching baseball uses obscene language to describe the game, its players, and its rules. You need this person's point of view for your story. What can you do?

____

____

____

3. You've just seen one of the worst plays ever produced. You hated every minute of it. In thinking it over, you can't come up with a single positive comment. Your review is due at the end of the week. What do you do?

____

____

____

Name: ______________________________ Date: ______________

9.5 Taking Responsibility (continued)

4. In writing about a ring of students caught selling stolen tests, you get conflicting quotes about the number of tests stolen. One reliable source says it was over 10. All of the students admit to stealing only six tests. A teacher says at least five tests were stolen from her files. Rumors put the number close to 20. What do you report?

   ____

   ____

   ____

5. One of the people you interviewed about her part in a sports scandal asked that her information be kept off the record. You can't get the information from anyone else, and it's very important to the story. What do you do?

   ____

   ____

   ____

Name: ______________________________ Date: ____________

10.1 Being a Correspondent

Imagine that you've been hired as a correspondent for your local newspaper. They want you to submit two news or feature stories each week about events at your school.

On the lines below, write your ideas for school-based stories that you might write over the next two weeks (four stories). For each story idea, indicate your angle, ideas for sources, events you may need to attend, and why you think it's a good story to cover for your local audience.

Name: ______________________________ Date: ______________

10.2 Being a Stringer

Imagine that you've been hired as a stringer for a large city daily nearby. They want you to write reviews—from a teen's perspective—for their weekend entertainment section.

In the space below, write a review of a product or performance, such as a recent movie, play, live music performance, music recording, or computer game. Provide a strong point of view that will speak to your age group. But remember that you're writing for a major publication with a broader audience as well.

Follow the guidelines for writing reviews on pages 116–117 of the *Handbook*. Use your editing skills to shape and refine your review.

Name: ______________________________ Date: ______________

10.3 Planning a Yearbook

Work with one or two other students to answer the questions below.

1. Look through old copies of your school's yearbook. What themes and patterns do you find?

2. Brainstorm and then choose a theme phrase and logo for the yearbook. Your theme phrase should serve as an advertising slogan for what's happening in your school this year. For example, if your school is introducing new classes and scheduling, your theme might be "A Fresh Twist." Your logo should combine the phrase with a simple illustration that will look good whether it's large or reduced to a small size.

3. What different sections will you have? How might each have a title that spins off the main theme?

Name: ______________________________ Date: ______________

10.3 Planning a Yearbook (continued)

4. What do you think will be the busiest times of the year for the staff? Why?

____

____

____

5. Write an introduction to the yearbook that explains the theme. It doesn't have to be long. In fact, the copy should be spare. But it should also have plenty of energy and should leave readers wanting to read more.

____

____

____

____

____

____

Name: ______________________________ Date: ______________

10.4 Finding a Market for Your Writing

On the lines below, write a few paragraphs describing the type of magazine you might like to write for as well as any ideas you have for books you'd like to write (soon or someday).

Then use the writer's-market guides at your school or local library to determine which magazines and book publishers are looking for the type of writing you'd like to do. Take notes on your findings and attach them to this worksheet. You may photocopy and attach relevant pages from the directories you found, highlighting specific information.

Name: ______________________________ Date: ______________

10.5 Sampling: Internet Publishing

Surf the Internet to find web sites for publications that you think are well done. See if you can find some good on-line student publications. Keep in mind that you're looking for on-line *publications,* not personal home pages, business pages, or pages that present lists of links and other information on a single topic.

On the lines below, write the addresses of the web sites you've chosen and state why you think they're effective. Be prepared to discuss the web publications with others in class.

Name: ______________________________ Date: ______________

10.6 Copy Writing

Choose an organization in your community that interests you. Whether you choose a homeless shelter, an art museum, a youth center, or something else, make sure it's an organization you believe in. In the space below, create a slogan and ad copy for a flyer about your chosen organization. Indicate photos or art needed. Your writing should be clear, concise, and colorful. Look at other flyers for similar organizations to get ideas.

Slogan: ______________________________

Copy: ______________________________

Name: ____ Date: _______________

10.7 Writing a News Release

Imagine you are part of the public relations department of an organization in your community (it may be the same one you chose for Worksheet 10.6, Writing a Brochure). Your organization is having its annual fund-raiser. On the lines below, write a news release to be distributed to area newspapers and other media. Be sure to include the 5 W's and H. Include the name of the organization in the upper left-hand corner. Put the release date—for example, "For Immediate Release" or "For [date] Release" in the upper right-hand corner.

Name: ______________________________ Date: ______________

10.8 Broadcast Journalists and Print Journalists

Using the Venn diagram below, compare the skills required of broadcast journalists and print journalists. In one circle note skills that you think only broadcast journalists need; in the other note skills that only print journalists. Where the circles overlap, write the skills required of both.

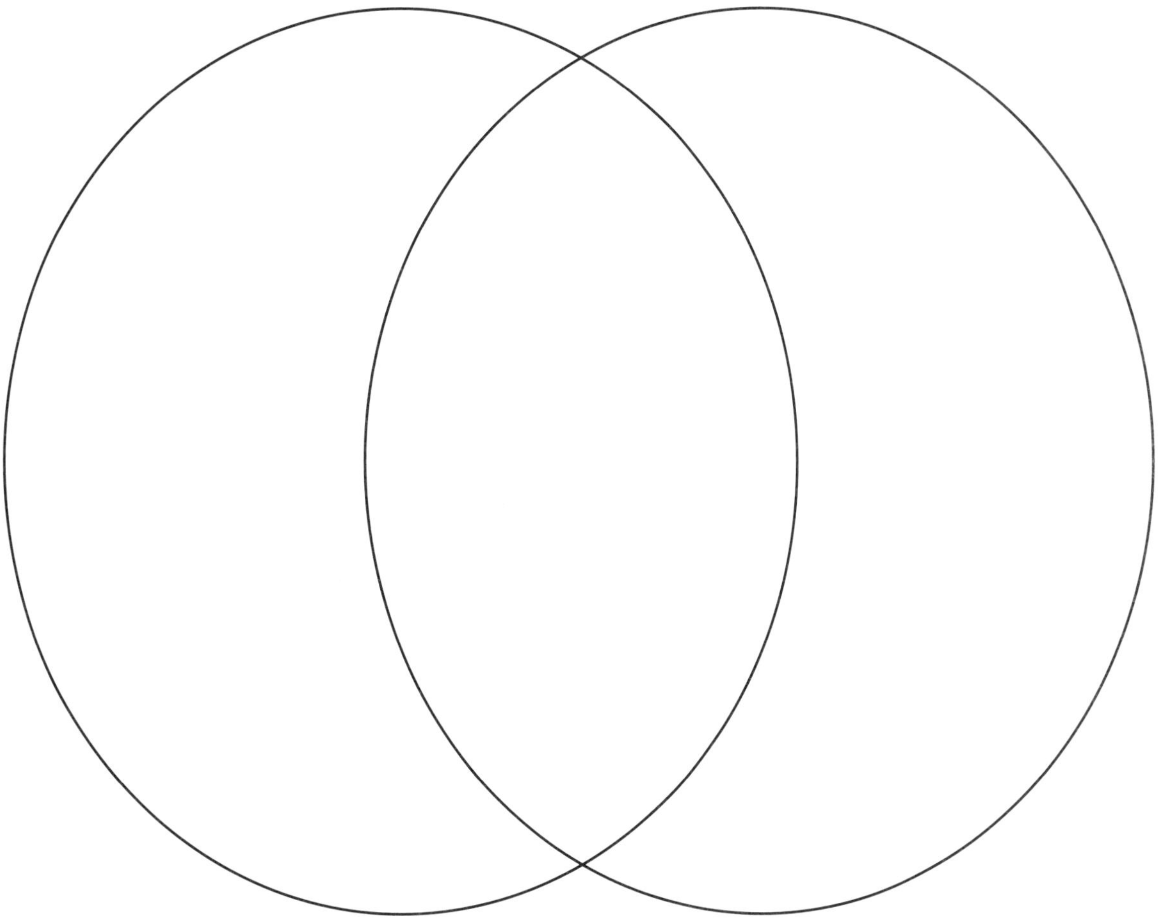

Name: ______________________________ Date: ______________

10.9 Videotaping a News Broadcast

Work with one or two other students to research, write, and videotape a news broadcast of several news briefs. Write your copy so that it reads clearly. Use graphics such as maps or illustrations if you like. The anchor, or reader, of the news should speak clearly, make eye contact with the camera, and present a poised appearance on camera. Be prepared to share your broadcast with others in your class.

Document who did what on your news crew and attach it, with your copy, to this worksheet. Write about the experience on the lines below, including any feedback you get from your classmates.